The Road To Life

The Road To Life

THE SEER

aldivan teixeira torres

Contents

1

The Road to Life
The Seer

The Road to Life

Author: The Seer

©2020- The Seer

All rights reserved.

Series: Cultivating Wisdom

This book, including all its parts, is copyrighted and cannot be reproduced without the author's permission, resold or downloaded.

The seer is a writer consolidated in several genres. So far, the titles have been published in dozens of languages. From an early age, he has always been a lover of the art of writing, having consolidated a professional career from the second half of 2013. He hopes, with his writings, to contribute to international culture, arousing the pleasure of reading in those who do not have the habit. Your mission is to win the hearts of each of your readers. In addition to literature, his main amusements are music, travel, friends, family and the pleasure of life itself. "For literature, equality, fraternity, justice, dignity and honor of the human being always" is his motto

Resume

The path
Knowing how to be critical
Law of return
A time of anguish
The plant-harvesting ratio
Give or not give the alms?
The act of teaching and learning
How to act in the face of treason
Love generates more love
Act on behalf of the poor, the excluded and subordinates
Final Message
The path of well-being
The path
The paths to God
The good masters and apprentices
Good practices for staying sober
The value through the example
The feeling in the universe
Feeling divine
Changing the routine
World inequality versus justice
The power of music
How to fight evil
I'm the incomprehensible
Experiencing problems
At work
Traveling
Seeking rights
Believe in full love
Knowing how to manage a relationship
The massage
The adoption of moral values
Having the spirit of a true friend

Actions to be observed
Care for feeding
Tips for living long and well
Dance
Fasting
The concept of God
Improvement steps
Characteristics of the mind
How am I supposed to feel?
The role of education
Conclusion
Winning by faith
Victory over spiritual and fleshly enemies
The man-God relationship
Believing in Yahweh in pain
Being an honest man of faith
The Christs
The mission of man
Be the Christ
The two paths
The choice
My experience
Destination
Kingdom of Light, October 1982
The mission
The meaning of vision
Authenticity in a corrupted world
Sadness in difficult times
Living in a corrupted world
As long as good exists the earth will remain
The Righteous will not be shaken
Be the exception
My fortress
The values

Seeking Inner Peace
The Creator God
True love
Recognize yourself sinner and limited
The influence of the modern world
How to integrate with the father
The importance of communication
The interdependence and wisdom of things
Don't blame anyone
Being part of a whole
Don't complain
See from another point of view
A truth
Think of the other
Forget the problems
Face birth and death as processes
Immortality
Have a proactive attitude
God is spirit
A vision of faith
Follow my commandments
The dead faith
Have another vision
From weakness comes strength
What to do in a delicate financial situation
Facing family problems
Overcoming a disease or even death
Meeting yourself
Sophia
Justice
The refuge at the right time
The seduction of the world versus the way of God
Getting to know Yahweh
The righteous and the relationship with Yahweh

The relationship with Yahweh
What you should do
I give you all my hope
Friendship
Forgiveness
Finding your way
How to live at work
Living with hard-tempered people at work
Preparing to have an autonomous work income
Analyzing options of specialization in studies
How to live in the family
What is Family
How to respect and be respected
Financial dependence
The importance of the example

The path

Walk with the good guys, and you'll have peace. Walk with the bad guys, and you'll be unhappiness. Tell me who you're hanging out with, and I'll tell you who you are. This wise saying reveals how important it is to be selective in friendships. However, I believe it's all a learning experience. You have to make mistakes to learn, or you have to experiment to know what you like. Experience is a primordial factor for the evolution of the human being since we are wandering beings subjected to a reality of atonement and evidence.

Knowing how to be critical

We are constantly evolving beings. It is normal to criticize yourself and always want to improve your performance in your everyday activities. But don't demand too much from yourself. Time teaches and matures your ideas. Divide your tasks in such a way that you have enough leisure. Overwhelmed mind produces nothing of convenient. There is the time of planting and harvesting.

It takes empathy and control. If your partner makes a mistake, give him good advice, but don't recreate him. Remember that we cannot judge the other because we are also imperfect and flawed beings. It would be a blind man guiding another blind man who would not bear fruit. Reflect, plan, and realize. They are the necessary pillars for success.

If you are a boss, demand skills from your subordinates, but also be understanding and human. A work environment loaded with heavy and negative vibrations only hinders our development. It takes cooperation, delivery, work, determination, planning, control and tolerance in the work environment. This is called labor democratization, an essential item in the conduct of business since our society is plural and multifaceted. The environment must therefore be a place of social inclusion.

Customers and consumers admire large companies that strive for inclusion and sustainability. This generates a highly positive image inside and outside the organization. In addition to this, values of unity, assiduousness, dignity and honor contribute to the perpetuity of the business. In this case, I recommend punctual meeting with highly qualified professionals such as: psychologist, human relations technician, administrators, successful managers, writers, health professionals among others.

Masters of life

We are on a great mission in front of a totally unequal crowd. Some have more knowledge and others have less knowledge. However, each of us can teach or learn. Wisdom is not measured by its age or its social condition, it is a divine gift. Then we can find a beggar who is wiser than a successful businessman. It is not measured by financial power, but by a construction of values that makes us more human. Success or failure is only a consequence of our acts.

Our first masters are our parents. So, it's true that our family is our base of values. Then we have contact with society and at school. All this reflects on our personality. While we always have the power of choice. Called free will, it is the condition of freedom of all beings and must be respected. I am free to choose my path, but I also have to bear the consequences. Remember, we only received what we plant. That's why you call it a good tree, it's the one that bears good fruit.

We are born with a predisposition to good, but often the environment brings us harm. A child in a state of repression and misery does not develop in the same way as a wealthy child. This is called social inequality, where few people have a lot of money and many people are poor. Inequality is the great evil of the world. It is a great injustice that brings suffering and damage to the portion of the less favored population. I think we need more social inclusion policies. We need jobs, income and opportunities. I think charity is a stunning act of love, but I think it's humiliating to live just that. We need work and decent conditions of survival. We need to hope for better days. How good it is to buy things with our work and not be discriminated against. We need to have everyone's opportunity, without any kind of discrimination. We need jobs for blacks, indigenous people, women, homosexuals, transsexuals, anyway, for everyone.

I think the way out of a new sustainability model would be the elite's joint work with the government. Less taxes, more financial incentives, less bureaucracy would help reduce inequality. Why does a person need billions in their bank account? This is totally unnecessary even if it is the fruit of your labor. We need to tax the great fortunes. We also need to collect the labor and tax debts of large companies to generate dividends. Why privilege the rich class? We are all citizens with rights and duties. We're the same before the law, but we're actually unequal.

Law of return
A TIME OF ANGUISH

When a time of anguish comes, and it seems that all the unjust are thriving, rest assured. Sooner or later, they will fall and the righteous will win. Yahweh's ways are unknown, but they are upright and wise, at no time will he abandon you even though the world condemns you. It does so that its name is perpetuated from generation to generation.

THE PLANT-HARVESTING RATIO

Everything you do on earth for your sake is being written in the book of life. Every council, donation, detachment, financial aid, kind words, compliments, cooperation in charitable works among others is a step towards prosperity and happiness. Do not think that helping the other the greatest good is for the assisted. On the contrary, your soul is the most benefited by your acts, and you can get higher flights. Have the awareness in you that nothing is free, the good we received today we plant in the past. Have you ever seen a house support itself without a foundation? So, too happens with each of our actions.

GIVE OR NOT GIVE THE ALMS?

We live in a world of cruel and full of swindlers. It is common for many people with good financial conditions to ask for alms to enrich, a disguised act of theft that sucks the already misgiving salary of workers. Faced with this everyday situation, many refuses to help in the face of a request for alms. Is this the best option?

It is best to analyze on a case-by-case basis, feel the person's intention. There are countless scourges on the street, there is no way to help everyone, that's true. But when your heart permits, help. Even if it is a fraud, sin will be in the intention of the other person. You've done your part, contributed to a less unequal and more humane world. Congratulations to you.

THE ACT OF TEACHING AND LEARNING

We are in a world of atonement and trials, a world in constant change. To adapt to this environment, we find ourselves in a rich teaching-learning process that is reflected in all environments. Take this opportunity, absorb the good things and deny the bad ones so that your soul can evolve on the path toward the father.

Always be grateful. Thank God for your family, friends, journey companions, life teachers, and all those who believe in you. Give back to the universe some of your happiness by being an apostle of good. It's really worth it.

HOW TO ACT IN THE FACE OF TREASON

Be careful with people, don't trust so easily. False friends won't think twice and deliver their secret in front of everyone. When this occurs, the best thing to do is to step back and put things in their proper places. If you can and have evolved enough, forgive. Forgiveness will free your soul from resentment, and then you will be ready for new experiences. Forgiving does not mean forgetting because once you've broken your trust, you won't come back.

Keep in mind the law of return which is the fairest law of all. Anything you do wrong to the other will return with interest for you to pay. So, don't worry about the harm they've done to you, you'll be there for your enemies, and God will act righteously by giving you what everyone deserves.

LOVE GENERATES MORE LOVE

Blessed be he who experienced love or passion. It is the most sublime feeling there is that comprises giving, renunciation, surrender, understanding, tolerance and detachment from the material. However, we do not always have a feeling reciprocated by the loved one and that is when pain and dismay occur. There is a time required to weigh it and respect this period. When you feel better, move on and don't regret anything. You loved it, and as a reward, God will show the other person a way, that he or she will go their way forward as well. There is a high probability that she will be rejected by others to pay for the suffering caused. This restarts a vicious cycle, where we never have whom we really love.

ACT ON BEHALF OF THE POOR, THE EXCLUDED AND SUBORDINATES

Seek to help homeless people, orphans, prostitutes, the abandoned and the unloved. Your reward will be great because they cannot repay your goodwill.

In a company, school, family and society in general treat everyone with equality regardless of their social class, religion, ethnicity, sexual choice, hierarchy or any specificity. Tolerance is a great virtue for you to have access to the highest heavenly courts.

FINAL MESSAGE

Well, that's the message I wanted to give. I hope these few lines will enlighten your heart and make you a better person. Remember: It's always time to change and do good. Join us in this chain of good for a better world. See you next story.

The path of well-being

THE PATH

The human being in all his consciousness has two dimensions to be observed: the way he sees himself and the way in which he is seen by society. The biggest mistake is that he can make is trying to fit a standard of society like ours. We live in a world that is mostly prejudiced, unequal, tyranny, cruel, evil, full of betrayals, falsehood, and material illusions. Absorbing good teachings and being authentic is the best way to feel accepting yourself.

Learning and knowing oneself better, relying on good values, liking yourself and others, valuing family and practicing charity are ways to find success and happiness. In this trajectory there will be falls, victories, sorrows, happiness, moments of leisure, war and peace. The important thing in all this is to keep yourself with faith in yourself and a greater force whatever your belief.

It is essential to leave all the bad memories behind and move on with your life. Rest assured that Yahweh God prepares good surprises in which you will feel the true pleasure of living. Have optimism and perseverance.

THE PATHS TO GOD

I am the son of the father, the one who came to help this dimension in a truly consistent evolution. Here when I arrived, I found a humanity totally messed up and diverted from my father's primary goal in creating it. Today, what we see most often are petty, selfish, unbelieving people of God, competitive, greedy and envious. I feel sorry for these people and I try to help them in the best way I can. I can show through my example the qualities my father really wants them to cultivate: Solidarity, understanding, cooperation, equality, fraternity, companionship, mercy, justice, faith, claw, persistence, hope, dignity and above all love among beings.

Another major problem is human pride in being part of a more favored group or class. I tell you; this is not a gall before God. I am telling you that you have open arms and hearts to receive your children regardless of your race, color, religion, social class, sexual orientation, political party, region or any specificity. Everyone is equal in matters before their father. However, some are more benefited by their works and pleasant soul.

Time runs fast. So, don't miss the opportunity to collaborate for a better and fairer universe. Help the afflicted, the sick, the poor, friends, enemies, acquaintances, strangers, family, strangers, men and women, children, young or old, in short, help without expecting retribution. Great will be your reward before the father.

THE GOOD MASTERS AND APPRENTICES

We are in a world of atonement and evidence. We are interdependent beings and lacking affection, love, material resources and attention. Each one throughout their lives is gaining experience and transmitting something good to those closest to them. This mutual exchange is essential to reach a state of full peace and happiness. Understanding one's own, understanding the pain of others, acting for justice, transforming concepts and experiencing the freedom that knowledge provides is priceless. It's a good that no one can steal from you.

During my life I had great teachers: My spiritual and carnal father, my mother with her sweetness, teachers, friends, family in general, acquaintances, co-workers, the guardian, Angel, The Hindu, the priestess, Renato (my adventure partner), Philip Andrews (A man marked by a tragedy), so many other characters who with his personality marked my story. In the setback of history, I mentored my nephews and all humanity through my books. I've done both roles well, and I'm looking for my identity. The key to the question is to leave a good seed for as Jesus said: the righteous will shine like the sun in their father's kingdom.

GOOD PRACTICES FOR STAYING SOBER

There are different ways to see the world and get used to it. In my particular case, I could maintain stability after a long time of internal spiritual preparation. From my experience, I can give tips on how to orient myself in the face of the inconstancy of life: Do not drink alcohol, do not smoke, do not use any drugs, work, occupy yourself with pleasurable activity, go out with friends, walk, travel in good company, eat and dress well, get in touch with nature, escape the rush and animation, rest your mind, listen to music, read books, fulfill domestic obligations, be faithful to your values and beliefs, respect the elders, take care of the instruction of the younger ones, be pious, understanding and tolerant, gather to your spiritual group, pray, have faith and not themes. Somehow fate will open the good doors for you and then find your way. A lot of luck is what I wish for everyone.

THE VALUE THROUGH THE EXAMPLE

Man is reflected through his works. This wise saying demonstrates exactly how we must act to achieve bliss. It is of no use to man to have consolidated values if he does not put them into practice. More than good intentions we need consolidated attitudes for the world to then be transformed.

THE FEELING IN THE UNIVERSE

Learn to know yourself, to value yourself more, and to cooperate for the good of others. Much of our problems stem from our fears and shortcomings. Knowing our weaknesses, we can fix them and plan in the future to improve as a human being.

Follow your ethics without forgetting the right of those who are at your side. Always be impartial, fair and generous. The way you treat the world will have as retribution success, peace and tranquility. Don't be too picky with yourself. Try to enjoy every moment of life from a learning perspective. Next time, you'll know exactly how to act.

FEELING DIVINE

Nothing is by chance and everything that exists in the universe has its importance. Be happy for the gift of life, for the opportunity to breathe, walk, work, see, hug, kiss and give love. No one is an isolated piece; we are part of the gear of the universe. Try doing simple mental connection exercises. In your moments off, go to your room, sit on your bed, close your eyes and reflect on yourself and the universe itself. As you relax, your problems will be left behind, and you will notice the approach to the divine link. Try to focus on the light at the end of the tunnel. This light brings you the hope that it is possible to change, erase the mistakes of the past, forgive yourself and make peace with enemies by making them friends. Forget the fights, the resentment, the fear and the doubts. All this just gets in your way. We are most active when we understand each other's side and have the ability to move on. Thank you, that you are healthy and that you still have time to resolve the pending issues.

We are sons of the father; we were created to help the planet evolve and also be happy. Yes, we can have it all if we are worthy of it. Some are happy alone, others alongside a companion, others by engaging in a religion or creed, and others by helping others. Happiness is relative. Never forget also that there will be days of despair and darkness and that it is at this moment that your faith must be more present. In the face of pain, finding a way out is sometimes quite complicated.

However, we have a God who never abandons us even if others do. Talk to him and then you'll understand things better.

CHANGING THE ROUTINE

The world today has become a great race against time for survival itself. We often spend more time at work than with our families. This is not always healthy, but it becomes necessary. Take the days off to change your routine a little. Go out with friends, spouse, go to parks, theaters, climb mountains, go swimming in the river or at sea, go visit relatives, go to the movies, the football stadium, read books, watch TV, surf the internet and make new friends. We need to change the routine view of things. We need to know a little of this vast world and enjoy what God has left. Think that we are not eternal, that at any moment something can happen, and you are no longer among us. So, don't leave for tomorrow what you can do today. At the end of the day, thank you for the opportunity to be alive. This is the greatest gift we've received.

WORLD INEQUALITY VERSUS JUSTICE

We live in an insane, competitive and unequal world. The feeling of impunity, hopelessness, avarice and indifference is preponderant. Everything Jesus has taught in the past most of the time is not being put into practice. So, what's the point of him fighting so hard for a better world if we don't value it?

It is effortless to say that you understand the pain of the other, sometimes have solidarity and compassion seeing an image on the internet or even in the street in front of an abandoned minor. It's hard to have attitude and try to change this story. Undoubtedly, the misery of the world is very great, and we have no way to help everyone. God won't demand that from you at trial. However, if you can at least help your neighbor will already be of good size. But who's our next one? It's your unemployed brother, it's your sad neighbor for losing his wife, it's his co-worker in need of your guidance. Every act of yours, however small it is counts, in the aspect of evolution. Remember: We are what our works are.

Always try to help. I will not demand your perfection; this is something that does not exist in this world. What I want is for you to love your neighbor, my father and yourself. I'm here to show you again how great my love for humanity is even though it doesn't deserve it. I suffer greatly from human misery and will try to use it as an instrument of my goodwill. However, I need your permission to be able to act in your life. Are you ready to really live my will and that of my father? The answer to this question will be a definitive milestone in its existence.

THE POWER OF MUSIC

Something very relaxing and that I highly recommend for the reach of peace and human evolution is to listen to music. Through the lyrics and melody, our mind travels and feels exactly what the author wants to go through. Often this frees us from all the evils we carry during the day. The pressure of society is so great that we are often struck by the negative and envious thoughts of others. Music frees us and comforts us by clearing our minds completely.

I have an eclectic taste for music. I like Rock, Funk, Brazilian popular music, international, romantic, country or any good quality music. Music inspires me and often writing I hear them of quiet music preferences. Do this too, and you'll see a big difference in your quality of life.

HOW TO FIGHT EVIL

We have lived a duality in the universe since the fall of the great dragon. This reality is reflected here on earth as well. On the one hand, honest people wanting to live and cooperate and other bastards who seek the misfortune of others. While the force of evil is black magic, the power of good is prayer. Don't forget to recommend yourself to your father at least once a day so that the force of darkness doesn't hit you.

As Jesus taught, do not fear the man who can take his life from his body, a theme that can condemn his soul. Through free will, you can simply reject the onslaught of enemies. The choice for good or evil is yours alone. When you sin, don't justify yourself. Recognize your mistake and try not to miss anymore.

An attitude I had in my life completely changed my relationship with the universe and with God. I wished that the lord's will would accomplish in my life and then the Holy Spirit might act. From then on, I only had success and happiness because I am obedient. Today I live in full communion with my creator, and I am pleased for that. Remember that it's your choice.

I'M THE INCOMPREHENSIBLE

Who am I? Where did I come from? Where am I going to go? What's my goal? I'm the incomprehensible. I'm the spirit of the north that blows from there to here without direction. Furthermore, I am love, the faith of the righteous, the hope of children, I am the helping hand of the afflicted, I am the advice well given, I am your conscience alerting danger, I am the one who animates the soul, I am forgiveness, I am reconciliation, I am understanding and will always believe in your recovery even before sin. I am David's sapling, the first and last, I am god's providence that creates the worlds. I am the little dreamy bud of the northeast destined to conquer the world. Furthermore, I am Divine to the most intimate, the seer or simply the son of God by right. I came down at my father's behest to save them again from the darkness. Before me there is no power, authority or royalty for I am the King of Kings. I am your God of the impossible that can transform your life. Always believe that.

EXPERIENCING PROBLEMS

As being divine I can do everything and in human form I live with weaknesses like any other. I was born in a world of oppression, poverty, hardship and indifference. I understand your pain like no one else. Furthermore, I can see deep in your soul your doubts and your fear of what may come. Aware of that, I know exactly how best to face them.

I'm your best friend, the one who's by your side every hour.

We may not know each other, or I'm not present physically, but I can act through people and in spirit. I want the best for your life. Don't be rebellious and understand the reason for the failure. The reason is that something is prepared for something better, something you never imagined. I learned this from my experience. I experienced an intense moment of despair in which no living being has helped me. Near total wear and tear, my father rescued me and showed his immense love. I want to repay and do the same to the rest of humanity.

I know exactly what's going on in your life. Furthermore, I sometimes know it feels like no one understands you, and it just feels like you're alone. In these moments, seeking a logical explanation does not help. The truth is, there's a big difference between human love and mine. While the former is almost always involved in a game of interests, my love is sublime and supreme. I raised you, provided you with the gift of life, and I dawn every day by your side through my angel. I care about you and your family. Furthermore, I feel very sorry when you suffer, and it's rejected. Know that in me, you will never get a negative. Meanwhile, I ask you to understand my plans and accept them. I have created the whole universe and I know more than you the best way. To this some call it a destination or predestination. As much as everything seems wrong, everything has a meaning and moves towards success if you are deserved.

Here is among you someone who loved and who loves. My eternal love will never pass away. My love is full and has no demands. Just have consolidated values of a good man. Do not want to put words of hatred, racism, prejudice, injustice or contempt in me. I'm not this God they paint. If you want to meet me, learn through my children. Peace and good to all.

AT WORK

It's not good that the man has an unoccupied mind. If we cultivate idleness, we will not stop thinking about the problems, the restlessness, the fears, our shame, the disappointments, the sufferings and the inconstancy of the present and the future. God left man the inheritance of work. Besides being a matter of survival, working fills our innermost void. The feeling of being useful to yourself and to society is unique.

Having the possibility of being in a job, growing professionally, strengthening the relationships of friendship and affection and of evolving as a human being is a great gift the result of their more tender efforts. Be happy about it in times of crisis. How many fathers and mothers didn't want to be in your shoes? The reality in our country is of increasing unemployment, inequality, inanity, indifference and political indifference.

Do your part. Maintain a healthy environment at work where you spend much of your day. However, don't have so much expectation and don't confuse things. Friends usually you find in life and at work only colleagues except rare exceptions. The important thing is to strictly comply with your obligations that involves attendance, punctuality, promptness, efficiency, responsibility and dedication. Be an example of conduct inside and outside your breakdown.

TRAVELING

God is wonderful, powerful and unmatched. For his great love, he wanted to create things and through his word they existed. All material, immaterial, visible, and invisible things yield glory to the creator. Among these things is the man. Considered a tiny point in the universe, it can see, feel, interact, perceive and realize. We're here to be happy.

Take advantage of the opportunities that life gives you and get to know a little of this universe. You will be enchanted by the small and large natural works. Feel the fresh air, the sea, the river, the forest, the mountains and yourself. Reflect on your attitudes and experiences throughout your life. Believe me this will give you quality of life and a sense of indescribable peace. Be happy now. Don't leave it for later because the future is uncertain.

SEEKING RIGHTS

Be a full citizen living your rights completely. Know exactly your duties and obligations. If they are violated, you may seek redress in court. Even if your request is not fulfilled, your conscience will be clear and ready to move on. Remember that the only righteousness that does not fail is the divine and with the right attitudes your blessing will come.

BELIEVE IN FULL LOVE

Today, we live in a world dominated by interest, wickedness and lack of understanding. It is demotivating to realize that what we really want for us does not exist or is absolutely rare. With the devaluation of being and true love, we run out of alternatives. I have suffered enough from the challenges of life and from my experience I still believe in a hope even if perhaps distant. I believe there is a spiritual father in another plane observing all our deeds. His works throughout his career will accredit future happiness alongside a special person. Be optimistic, persevering, and have faith.

KNOWING HOW TO MANAGE A RELATIONSHIP

Love is Divine. Being this feeling conceptualized as the want the well-being of the other individual. In the process of reaching this stage, you need to know. Knowledge enchants, disenchants or amorphous. Knowing how to deal with each of these phases is the task of the good administrator. Using a figure of language, affection can be compared to a plant. If we water it frequently, it will grow and give good fruit and flowers. If we despise her, she withered, decays and ends. Being in a relationship can be something positive or negative depending on whom we're with. Living together for a couple is the great challenge of modern times. Now that love alone is not enough to perpetuate a union is something that involves broader factors. However, he is a powerful refuge in times of anguish and despair.

THE MASSAGE

Massage is a great exercise that can be done. Who is the receiver having the opportunity to experience the pleasure caused by the relaxation of muscles? However, care must be taken not to exaggerate the proportionality of the friction between the hands and the area worked. You can take even better advantage of that when there's an exchange between two people who love each other.

THE ADOPTION OF MORAL VALUES

Good guidance is essential to develop a sense capable of establishing sincere, realistic, well-enjoyed and true connections. As the saying goes, the family is the basis of everything. If within it, we are good parents, children, brothers and companions we will also be outside it.

Practice an ethics of values capable of directing you to the path of well-being. Think of yourself, but also of the other's right always with respect. Try to be happy even though your mind weakens and discourages you. No one really knows what happens if they don't act and try. The most that can happen is a failure, and they were made to train us and make us real winners.

HAVING THE SPIRIT OF A TRUE FRIEND

When Jesus was on earth, he left us a model of behavior and an example to follow. His greatest act was the surrender on the cross for our sins. In this lies the value of a true friendship, donating your life for the other. Who really in your life would do that for you? Take a good look. If your response is positive, value this person and love them sincerely because this feeling is rare. Don't ruin this relationship for anything. Reciprocate with deeds and words a little of this great love and be happy.

ACTIONS TO BE OBSERVED

1. Do to others what you would like them to do to you. This includes being friendly, charitable, kind, generous, and striving not to hurt others. You have no dimension of what it is to suffer because of misplaced words. Use this power only to provide good

and comfort to others because we do not know what fate holds for us.

2. Be the enemy of lies and always walk with the truth. As much as it does, it's better to confess everything that happened. Don't justify yourself or soften the news. Be clear.
3. Do not steal what is from the other and do not cross in the way of the lives of others. Be fair on payments and account ability. Do not cultivate envy, slander, or falsehood with others.
4. We are all part of a whole known as God, destiny or cosmic consciousness. To maintain harmony, complicity and communion in the relationship, a tremendous effort is needed to stay away from the things of the world. Always exercise good and your path will gradually be traced to heavenly father. Like I've been saying, don't be afraid of anything. Unlike what many religions paint, my father is not an executioner or a bigot, he exalts love, tolerance, generosity, equality and friendship. Everyone has his place in my kingdom if he earns it.
5. Have a simple and safe life. Do not accumulate material goods without necessity and do not give in to extravagances. Everything has to be in the right measure. If you are rich or wealthy, always practice the art of donation and charity. You don't know the good this is going to do for yourself.
6. Keep body, soul and heart clean. Do not give in to the temptations of lust, gluttony or laziness.
7. Cultivate optimism, love, hope, faith and perseverance. Never give up on your dreams.
8. Whenever you can engage in community social projects. Each action for the favored minors will increase their treasure in heaven. Prefer this to power, money, influence, or social status.
9. Get used to valuing culture in its various manifestations. Go sightseeing with friends, cinema, theater and read inspiring books. The magical world of literature is a rich and diverse world that will bring you plenty of entertainment.
10. Meditate and reflect on your present and future. The past no

longer matters and even if your sin is as scarlet, I could forgive and show you my true love.

CARE FOR FEEDING

Taking care of our bodies is essential for us to live well. One of the basic and many important items is food. Adopting a balanced diet is the best way to avoid diseases. Acquire healthy habits and eat foods rich in vitamins, minerals, fibers and proteins. It is also important to eat only what is necessary for survival avoiding waste.

TIPS FOR LIVING LONG AND WELL

1. Always keep body and mind active.
2. Dating.
3. Cultivate your belief regarding others.
4. To have solid and generous values of social coexistence.
5. Eat moderately.
6. Have an appropriate exercise routine.
7. Sleep well.
8. Be sensible.
9. Wake up early.
10. Travel a lot.

DANCE

Dance is a critical exercise for the well-being of the individual. Helps fight aging, in back problems and locomotion, increases positivity. Integrating with each melody is not always an easy, but pleasurable and rewarding task. Have a habit in this exercise and try to be happy.

FASTING

Fasting is appropriate on holy days or when we make promises to help souls who are in trouble in the spirit world. However, once finished, it is recommended to recompose the forces by ingesting healthy and diverse foods.

THE CONCEPT OF GOD

God has not begun and will have no end. It is the result of the union of the creative forces of good. It is present in all the works of his creation communicating with them through the mental reflexive process what many call the "Inner Self".

God cannot be defined in human words. But if I could, I would say that it is love, brotherhood, give, charity, justice, mercy, understanding, justice and tolerance. God is willing to accept him into his kingdom if you deserve it. Remember something critical: You are only entitled to rest in the kingdom of heaven who rested from your works your brethren.

IMPROVEMENT STEPS

The earth is a world of atonement and evidence for people to progress. This stage of our existence must be marked by our good deeds so that we can live a satisfactory spiritual dimension. By reaching the fullness of perfection, the human being becomes part of the cosmic dimension or simply conceptualized as God.

CHARACTERISTICS OF THE MIND

1. Good desire should be encouraged and put effectively into practice.
2. Thought is a creative force that must be freed for the creative spirit to flourish.
3. Dreams are signs of how we see the world. They can also be messages from the gods relates the future. However, it is necessary to remain in reality to achieve concrete results.
4. Discernment, knowledge, and detachment from material things must be worked in the minds of all who seek evolution.
5. Feeling part of the universe is the result of a process of improvement and consciousness. Know how to recognize your inner voice.

HOW AM I SUPPOSED TO FEEL?

Thank you for the gift of life and for all that your father has given you. Every achievement, every day lives must be celebrated as if another did not exist. Do not belittle yourself and know how to recognize your role in the dimension of the cosmos. My parents see them with a look of greatness despite their limitation and disbelief. Make yourself worthy of the good things.

Make like the little dreamer of the inland of Pernambuco known as Divine. Despite all the challenges and difficulties imposed by life, he never ceased to believe in a greater force and in his possibilities. Always believe in hope because God loves us and wants what is best for us. However, try to do your part in this process. Be active in your projects and dreams. Live each step fully and if it fails do not be discouraged. Victory will come by deserving.

THE ROLE OF EDUCATION

We are beings ready to evolve. From conception, childhood and even inclusion in the school itself we can learn and relate to others. This interaction is critical for our development in general. It is at this point that teachers, parents, friends and everyone we know plays a key role in building a personality. We must absorb the beneficial things and reject the evil ones by tread the right path toward the father.

CONCLUSION

I close here this first texts searching for knowing the religions. I hope that from my point of view you may have assimilated good teachings and if it helps even if it is only a person I will give as well given the time used to make. A hug to all, success and happiness.

Winning by faith
VICTORY OVER SPIRITUAL AND FLESHLY ENEMIES

Thus, says Yahweh: "To the righteous, those who rightly follow my commandments by practicing the daily art of good, I promise constant protection before my enemies. Even if a multitude or even all hell throws itself against you, you will fear no evil for I sustain you. By my name, ten thousand will fall to your right and a hundred me to your left, but nothing will happen to you, for my name is Yahweh."

This emblematic message from God is enough to leave us calm in the face of the wrath of enemies in any situation. If God is for us, who will be against us? In fact, there is no one greater than God anywhere in the universe. Everything that is written in the book of life will happen and surely, your victory will come, brother. The triumph of the unjust is made straw, but the wheat will remain forever. So, let's have more faith.

THE MAN-GOD RELATIONSHIP

Man was given the administration of the land so that he could make it bear fruit and prosper. As Jesus taught us, our relationship with God must be from father to son, and as a result, we are not ashamed to approach him even if sin makes him fearful. Yahweh cherishes the good heart, the hardworking man, the one who strives to improve always so that he can follow the path of permanent evolution.

At the moment of sin, it is best to reflect on what caused it so that the error cannot be repeated once again. Seeking alternative paths and looking for new experiences always adds to our curriculum making us more prepared people for life.

The main point of all this is to open your life to the action of the Holy Spirit. With his help, we can get to a level that we can say is connected with good things. This is called communion, and it is necessary and delivered and passion ed so that it can be lived fully. Giving up the things of the bodily world and denying evil within you are necessary and effective conditions to be born again in a changing world. We will be the mirror of the risen Christ.

BELIEVING IN YAHWEH IN PAIN

We live in a world of atonement and proof, which constantly makes us in pain. We suffer for a lost or unrequited love, suffer for the loss of a family member, suffer for financial problems, suffer for the misunderstanding of the other, suffer because of the violence caused by human wickedness, we suffer silently because of our weaknesses, longing, diseases and fear of death, we suffer for defeats and sad days when we wish to disappear.

My brother, since pain is inevitable for those who live in this world, we have to cling to Yahweh and his son Jesus Christ. The latter felt on the skin as a man all kinds of uncertainties, fears, misfortunes and yet never gave up being happy. Let us also be so, living every day with the feeling that you can do better and with a chance of progression. The secret is to always move on and ask him for help to carry our crosses. The omnipotent will reward your sincerity and conversion and transform your life into a sea of delights. It is not a question of ensuring the exclusion of pain, but of knowing how to live together in a way that they do not affect our good mood. And so, life can go on without major problems.

BEING AN HONEST MAN OF FAITH

The true Christian follows the example of Jesus in all circumstances. In addition to the essential commandments, you have a notion of the gospel, of life itself, of evil, and of the danger of the world, and you know the best way to act. The Christian must be an example of a citizen because there are rules to be followed and observed in the social set. One thing is faith and another thing is respect for your partner.

What Yahweh wants is for man to be his citizen too and not just the world. For this, one must be a good father, a good son, a good husband, a faithful friend, a servant dedicated in prayer, a man or woman who lives for work because idleness is the devil's workshop. Committed to the issue of Yahweh, the human being can take an important step towards being happy and finally *win by faith*! A big hug to all and see you next time.

The Christs

THE MISSION OF MAN

The earth was created to house life frequent as well as other stars scattered throughout the countless parts of the universe. Yahweh God, the consolidated love, wanted by strength, power, sweetness and grace to create humans, special creatures that have the prerogative to be his image and likeness.

But the fact that it's their image and likeness doesn't mean they have the same essence. While Yahweh possesses all the predicates of perfection man is flawed and sinful innately itself. God thus wanted to demonstrate his greatness, he loved us so much that he gave us free will by providing the key elements so that we may find for ourselves the path of happiness.

We conclude that perfection on earth has never been achieved since forever, which puts down some ancient legends of certain religions. We live duality, a fundamental condition for existing as a human being.

Now comes the question: What is the meaning of the creation of the universe and life itself? Yahweh and his plans are unknown to most people many of them do not even realize what happens around them. We can say that my father lives forever and ever, fathered two children, the prehuman Jesus and Divine, created the celestial stars being the first of them called "kalenquer". On this planet with aspects similar to that of the present earth, created the angels who are the second in order of universal importance. After that, he traveled through the universe to continue the mystery of creation, leaving his authority in the hands of Jesus, the Divine, and Michael (a most dedicated servant). This was about fifteen billion years ago.

From this time to the present, the universe was transformed in such a way that the initial creation is not even recognized. The meaning of life that is one of cooperation, unity, charity, love, donation and liberation has turned into dispute, envy, falsehood, enmity, crime, devastation of natural resources, love of money and power, individualism and the search for victory at all costs.

That's where I want to get to. I am the son of spiritual Yahweh and I came to earth to accomplish a critical mission. I want to call my brothers to my father's bounty and my kingdom. If you accept my invitation, I promise a constant dedication to your causes and supreme happiness. What does God require of you for this?

BE THE CHRIST

About two thousand years ago, the earth had the privilege of receiving God's firstborn. Known as Jesus Christ was sent by his father to bring the true word of God and redeem our sins. By his example, during his thirty-three years of life, Jesus dug the fundamental foundations of the perfect man who pleases God. Jesus came to clarify fundamental points in man's relationship with God.

The main point of the Messiah's life was his act of courage in surrendering himself to the cross by serving as a sacrifice for sinful humanity. "The true friend is the one who gives his life for the other unreservedly and Christ was a living example of it."

Surrendering, giving up for oneself by the brother, keeping the explicit and implicit commandments in the holy books, and doing good are always requirements to inherit the kingdom of God. This is the kingdom of Jesus, mine and all the souls of good, each in his deserved place.

Cultivate healthy, pleasurable and human values by assisting in the continuous evolution of the universe, and you will be planting a good seed towards the eternal kingdom. Stay away from bad influences and don't support some of your practices. Know how to discern good from evil. Be prudent and cautious.

The world we live in is a world of appearances where it is worth having more than being. Do it differently. Be the exception and value what it's really worth. Gather treasures in the sky where thieves don't steal or the moth and rust corrode.

After all that has been spoken with good placements, it is up to a personal reflection and a careful analysis on your part. It is your free choice to integrate or not into this kingdom, but if by chance your decision is a yes feel embraced by me and by all the heavenly forces. We will make this world a better world by promoting good and peace forever. Be one of the "Christs". In the future world, god willing, we will be together with the father in complete harmony and pleasure. See you next time. Yahweh is with you.

The two paths
THE CHOICE

The earth is a natural environment where humans have been placed to interact with each other, learning and teaching according to their experiences. By force of free will, the human being is always faced with situations that require decision-making. At this time, there is no magic formula of resolution but analysis of alternatives that do not always bring satisfactory results.

The mistakes made in these choices make us have a more critical spirit and a more open mind so that in the future we will have more hits on future choices. It is the so-called experience of because that is only achieved over time.

It is obvious throughout our trajectory on Earth that there are two strands that act in the universe: one malignant and one benign. Although no one is completely bad or good, our preponderant actions are who will decide our side in this dispute.

MY EXPERIENCE

I am the son of spiritual Yahweh, known as Messiah, Divine, son of God, or simply seer. I was born in a village in the interior of the Northeast and this gave me the opportunity to get in touch with the worst ills of humanity.

Choices certainly have a great weight in our lives and especially on our personality. I am the son of farmers, I was raised with good values and always followed them to the letter. I grew up impoverished, but I never lacked kindness, generosity, honesty, character, and love for others. Still, I wasn't saved from the bad weather.

My humble condition was a great scourge: I had no money for proper food, I did not have enough financial support in my studies, I was raised indoors with little social interaction. Although everything was difficult, I decided to fight this current searching for better days being my first important choice.

It wasn't easy at all. I suffered a lot, sometimes I lost hope, I gave up, but something deep down said that God supported me and prepared for me a path full of accomplishments.

At the very moment I had already given myself up, Yahweh God acted and delivered me. He adopted me as a son and resurrected me completely. From there he decided to live in me to transform the lives of the closest people.

Destination

KINGDOM OF LIGHT, OCTOBER 1982

The higher council met hastily to deliberate on an important question: What would be the spirit in charge of doing a job? One of the members took the word by pronouncing:

This job is critical. We need to choose someone who is of our complete confidence and who is prepared for the challenge of living on earth.

A heated discussion began between the members, each with his suggestion. As they did not reach an agreement, a quick vote was taken in which the elected representative was chosen. The spirit and the archangel were chosen for their protection.

Once the choice was made, Yahweh breathed and the spirits were sent to earth. One for a carnal body and one for a spiritual body, capable of surviving in the Earth's environment. This is how Divine and his Beloved Archangel arrived at earth and this is the similar process for every chosen human being. We all have the divine essence.

THE MISSION

Divine was born and raised amid astounding difficulties

somewhere in the back state of Pernambuco. An Intelligent and kind boy, has always been helpful to people in general. Even living with prejudice, misery and indifference never gave up on living. This is a great achievement in the face of political and social dismay in which the Northeast is inserted.

At the age of twenty-three, he lived with the first major financial and personal crisis. The problems led him to hit rock bottom, a period called the dark night of the soul, where he forgot God and his principles. Divine was falling non-stop on a bottomless cliff until something changed: The moment he was going to fall to the ground, the angel of Yahweh acted and freed him. Glory to Yahweh!

From there things began to change: He got a job, started college and started writing for therapy. Although the situation was still difficult, it had at least prospects for improvement.

Over the next four years, he completed college, changed jobs, stopped writing, and began a follow-up of his gift that was beginning to develop. Thus, began the saga of the seer.

THE MEANING OF VISION

Divine, the psychic, was treating himself in a private medical clinic with a famous parapsychologist. After a long treatment of six months finally came to a conclusion in the twelfth session. I will transcribe in summary the meeting below:

The St. Lawrence clinic was located in the center of Atalanta, backcountry of Pernambuco, a simple single-story building that was lost in the middle of the buildings of what was the capital of the backcountry. Divine had arrived at eight o'clock in the morning and as the doctor was immediately attended to. They both went to a private room and upon arriving there, Divine and doctor Hector Smith went head-to-head. The latter initiated the contact:

"I have good news. I developed a substance capable of transforming your spiritual electrical impulses into recordable photochemical units through my device. Depending on the results, we will reach a definitive conclusion.

"I am afraid. However, I wish to know the whole truth. Go ahead, Doctor.

"That's great. (Doctor Hector Smith)

With a sign brought Divine closer to a strange, circular, extensive device full of legs and wires. The device had liked a manual reader and gently the parapsychologist helped the young man to post his hands. The contact produced an intense shock in Divine and the results appeared on a viewfinder on the other side. Seconds later, Divine withdrew his hand and the doctor printed the result automatically.

In possession of the exam, he made a face of joy and returned to communicate:

" That's what I suspected. The visions you have are part of a natural process that is associated with another life. Your goal is just to guide you on the way. No contraindications.

"You mean I'm normal?

"Normal. Let's say you're special and unique on the planet. I think we can stop here. I'm satisfied.

"Thank you for your dedication and commitment in my cause. Friendship stays.

"I say the same thing. Good luck, son of God.

"To you too, goodbye.

"Bye.

That said, the two walked away outright. This day marked the revelation of Divine's visions and from there his life would follow the normal course.

With the revelation about the visions, Divine decided to continue in the work and resumed writing. Because of his gift, he called himself "The Seer" and began to build the literary series of the same name. Everything he had built so far showed him how worthy it was to work for a mission which had been entrusted by Yahweh himself.

Divine currently faces life with optimism. Even though life still preaches surprises to him, he persists in his goals by showing the value and faith of his person. He is an example that life and its difficulties have not destroyed.

The secret to its success lies in the belief in a greater force that drives everything that exists. Armed by this force, it is possible for man to overcome barriers and fulfill his destiny reserved in the lifelines.

Behold, the secret is this: "To live life with joy, with faith and hope. Transform some of his work for the whole universe and this is what Divine wants to do with his literature."

Good luck to him and to everyone who contributes to the culture of this country. Good luck to all and a loving hug.

Authenticity in a corrupted world
SADNESS IN DIFFICULT TIMES

The unrighteous perish and most often tries to place the blame on God and others. He does not realize that he is reaching the fruits of his labor, of his insanity in trying to live unruly and full of vices. The advice is that I do not worry about the success of others or envy him. Try to understand and find your own way through good works. Be honest, true and authentic above all else and then victory will come by deserving. Those who put their faith in Yahweh will come out disappointed in no time.

LIVING IN A CORRUPTED WORLD

The world today is very dynamic, competitive and full of violence. Being good these days is a real challenge. Often faithful experienced situations of betrayal, falsehood, envy, greed, hopelessness. My father seeks the reverse of this: kindness, cooperation, charity, love, determination, claw and faith. Make your choice. If you choose good, I promise your assistance in all its causes. I will ask my father for his dreams and he will listen to me because anything is possible to those who believe in God.

Cultivate solidified values that give you security and freedom. Your free will should be used for your glory and well-being. Choose to be an apostle of good. However, if you walk the path of darkness, I will not be able to help you. I'll be sad, but I'll respect any decision of yours. You're totally free.

In front of a sea of mud it is possible to filter good water and this is what I want to do with you. The past doesn't matter anymore. I will make you the man of the future: Happy, quiet and fulfilled. We will be happy forever before God the Father.

AS LONG AS GOOD EXISTS THE EARTH WILL REMAIN

Don't worry about the astronomical predictions about the end of life on Earth. Here's someone who's bigger than I. As long as there is good on earth life will remain for, so I desire. As time progresses, evil spreads on the earth contaminating my plantations. There will come a time when everything will be consummated and the separation between good and bad will be made. My kingdom will come upon you allowing the success of the faithful. On this day of the Lord will be paid the debts and the distribution of gifts.

My kingdom is a kingdom of delights where justice, the sovereignty of the father and common happiness will prevail. Everyone, big and small, will bow to his glory. Amen.

THE RIGHTEOUS WILL NOT BE SHAKEN

In the midst of storms and earthquakes, don't be me. Before you, there is a strong God who will sustain you. His authenticity, honor, faithfulness, generosity and kindness saved him. Their fraternal acts will lead them before the great, and you will be considered wise. In life, you have demonstrated enough to be justified and elevated. Alive!

BE THE EXCEPTION

Behold, I am righteous, I walk with integrity, I practice justice, I speak the truth, I do not slander, and I do no harm to others. I am the exception in a world where power, prestige, influence and the outside are most important. Therefore, I beg you, sir, protect me with your wings and your shield from all my enemies. May my authenticity bear fruit and place me among the great by deserving.

Those who despise righteousness and law know neither you nor your commandments. These will be taken from your barn and thrown at mo. in the lake of fire and brimstone where they will pay day and night without ceasing for their sins. Anyone who has ears who listen.

MY FORTRESS

My strength is my faith and my works testify to my goodness. I can't get enough of helping others of my own free will. I get nothing in return, my prize will come from heaven. On the Lord's day, when I gather in your arms, I will have proof that my efforts have been worth it.

My God is the God of the impossible and his name is Yahweh. He's done countless wonders in my life and treats me like a son. Blessed be your name. Also join us in this chain of good: Help the afflicted and the sick, help the needy, instruct the ignorant, give good advice, given to those who cannot repay, and then your reward will be great. His abode will be in the kingdom of heaven before me and my father, and then you will taste of true happiness.

THE VALUES

Cultivate the values proposed in the commandments and divine laws. Build your authenticity and suitability. It is well worth being an apostle of the beatitude on earth, you will receive wonderful gifts and graces that will make you happy. Good luck and success in your endeavors is what I desire with all my heart.

Seeking Inner Peace

THE CREATOR GOD

The universe and everything contained in it is the work of the Holy Spirit. The main characteristics of this being of splendid glory are: Love, fidelity, generosity, strength, power, sovereignty, mercy and justice. Good things when they reach perfection are assimilated by light and evil things are absorbed by darkness and lowered to lower degrees in the next incarnations. Heaven and hell are just stating of mind and not specific locations.

TRUE LOVE

Despite being a very great and powerful God, Yahweh takes care of each of his children personally or through his servants. He seeks our happiness at any cost. Like a mother or father, he supports us and helps us through difficult times by revealing an incomprehensible love for humans. Truly, on earth, we do not find in men this kind of pure and interest less love.

RECOGNIZE YOURSELF SINNER AND LIMITED

Arrogance, pride, self-confidence, illusion, and self-reliance are wicked enemies of humanity. Contaminated, they realize they are just a simple mass of dust. See and compare: I who created the suns, the black holes, the planets, the galaxies and the other stars, I don't brag about it the more you. Surrender to my power and take new attitudes.

THE INFLUENCE OF THE MODERN WORLD

The world today creates insurmountable barriers between man and the creator. We live surrounded by technology, knowledge, opportunities and challenges. In such a competitive world, man forgets the principal, his relationship with you. We must be like the ancient teachers who sought God unceasingly and have goals according to his will. Only in this way will success come to you.

HOW TO INTEGRATE WITH THE FATHER

I am life proof that God exists. The creator has transformed me from a little cave dreamer to an internationally recognized man. All this was possible because I integrated with my father. How was that possible? I renounced my individuality and let the forces of light act completely in my relations. Do as I do and enter our kingdom of delights where milk and honey flows, the paradise promised to the Israelites.

THE IMPORTANCE OF COMMUNICATION

Don't forget your religious obligations. Whenever you can or, at least once a day, pray fervently for you and the world. At the same time, your soul will be full of graces. Only those who are persistent can achieve the miracle.

THE INTERDEPENDENCE AND WISDOM OF THINGS

Look at the universe, and you will see that everything has a reason and a function even if small for the functioning of the whole. So, too it is with good that is a legion willing to fight for us. Feel the God inside you.

DON'T BLAME ANYONE

Do not blame fate or God for the result of your choices. On the contrary, reflect on them and try not to make the same mistakes. Each experience should serve as a learning to be assimilated.

BEING PART OF A WHOLE

Don't underestimate your work on earth. Have it as important to your evolution and that of others. Feel blessed to be part of the great theater of life.

DON'T COMPLAIN

No matter how much your problem, life tries to demonstrate that there are people in worse situations than yours. It turns out that much of our suffering is psychologically imposed by an idealized standard of health and well-being. We are weak, corruptible and naïve. But most people think you're an eternal superhero.

SEE FROM ANOTHER POINT OF VIEW

At the moment of distress, try to calm down. Notice the situation from another point of view and then what initially looks like a bad thing will certainly have its positives. Mentally, concentrate and try to take a new direction for your life.

A TRUTH

We are so drowned in our worries that we don't even realize the little gifts, miracles, and routine graces we receive from heaven. Be happy about that. With a little effort, you will be blessed even more because my father wishes you the best.

THINK OF THE OTHER

When your thoughts are high in concern for your brother, heaven feasts. Acting generously, our spirit is light and ready for higher flights. Always do this exercise.

FORGET THE PROBLEMS

Exercise creativity, reading, mentalization, meditation, charity, and conversation so that problems don't afflict your soul. Do not unload the heavy load you carry on others that has nothing to do with your personal problems. Make your day more free and more productive by being friendly.

FACE BIRTH AND DEATH AS PROCESSES

Being born and dying are natural events that must be viewed with serenity. The biggest concern is when one is alive to transform our attitudes into benefits primarily for others. Death is just a passage that leads us to a higher existence with prizes equivalent to our efforts.

IMMORTALITY

Man becomes eternal through his works and values. This is the legacy it will leave for future generations. If the fruits of the trees are more evil than the soul has no value to the creator being plucked and thrown into the outer darkness.

HAVE A PROACTIVE ATTITUDE

Don't just stand there. Seek knowledge of new cultures and meet new people. Your cultural baggage will be greater and consequently the results will be better. Be a wise man too.

GOD IS SPIRIT

Love can't be seen, you feel. So, too is with the Lord, we cannot see him, but we feel daily in our hearts his fraternal love. Give thanks every day for everything he does for you.

A VISION OF FAITH

Faith is something to be built in our daily life. Feed her with positive thoughts and firm attitudes toward her goal. Every step is important on this possible long journey.

FOLLOW MY COMMANDMENTS

The secret of success and happiness lies in following my commandments. There's no point in declaring in words that you love me if you don't follow what I say. Truly those who love me are those who comply with my law and vice versa.

THE DEAD FAITH

Every faith without works is truly dead. Some say that hell is full of good intentions and in this lies a great truth. It's no use being willing, but you must prove that you love me.

HAVE ANOTHER VISION

Not all suffering or defeat is completely evil. Every negative experience we experience brings continuous, strong and lasting learning into our lives. Learn to see the positive side of things, and you'll be happier.

From weakness comes strength

WHAT TO DO IN A DELICATE FINANCIAL SITUATION

The world is very dynamic. It is common to have phases of great prosperity owe back to periods of great financial difficulties. Most people when they're in a good time forget to keep fighting and the religious part. They simply feel self-reliant. This mistake can lead them to a dark abyss from which it will be difficult to escape. Right now, the important thing is to analyze the situation coldly, identify the solutions and go to fight with great faith in God.

With a religious support, you will be able to overcome obstacles and find ways of recovery. Don't blame yourself too much for your failed past. The important thing is to move forward with a new mindset formed allied to the grit and faith that will grow in your heart as you give your life to my father. Believe me, he will be the only salvation for all your problems.

Behold, the man has been told that all will be granted to him as long as he always walks the path of good. Therefore, strive to keep the commandments of the holy scriptures and the recommendations of the Saints. Don't be proud to the point of belittling them because by the example of life they could recognize God in the midst of the rubble. Think about it and good luck.

FACING FAMILY PROBLEMS

Since we were born, we have been integrated into the first human community that is the family. It is the basis of our values and reference in our relationships. Whoever is a good father, husband or son will also be a great citizen fulfilling his duties. Like any group, disagreements are inevitable.

I do not ask you to avoid friction, this is practically impossible. I ask you to respect each other, cooperate with each other and love each other. The family that is united will never end and together can conquer great things.

There is also a spiritual family consolidated in heaven: The Kingdom of Yahweh, Jesus and Divine. This kingdom preaches justice, freedom, understanding, tolerance, brotherhood, friendship and above all love. In this spiritual dimension there is no pain, weeping, suffering, or death. Everything has been left behind and the chosen faithful are clothed with a new body and a new essence. As it is written, "the righteous will shine like the sun in the kingdom of their father."

OVERCOMING A DISEASE OR EVEN DEATH

Physical illness is a natural process that occurs when something does not go well with our body. If the disease is not severe and is overcome, it plays the role of natural cleansing of the soul consolidating humility and simplicity. In suffering from the disease is that we are at a time of our smallness and at the same time we flood with the greatness of God that can do anything.

In case of fatal illness, it is the definitive passport to another plan and according to our conduct on the ground we are allocated in the specific plan. The possibilities are: Hell, limbo, heaven, city of men and purgatory. Each is intended for one of them according to their evolutionary line. At this point, we only get exactly what we deserve, no more, no less.

For those who stay on earth, the longing for family one's remains and life follows. The world is no stop for anyone, absolutely no one is irreplaceable. However, good works remain and bear witness to us. Everything will pass, except the power of God that is eternal.

MEETING YOURSELF

Where's my happiness? What to do to stay well on earth? That's what many people ask. There is not much of a trade secret, but the winning people are usually those who devote their time to the good of others and humanity. By serving others, they feel complete and are more willing to love, relate, and win.

Education, patience, tolerance, and fear of God are key elements in building a rare and admirable personality. By doing so, man will be able to find God and know exactly what he desires for his life. You may even think you're on the right track, but without these qualities you're just going to be a fake. You only love people who really give themselves up and who understands each other's side. Learn from me that I am pure, aware of my god-gods, God-care deeds dedicated to my projects, understanding, charitable, and loving. It will become special to my father and the world will be kept. Remember: No for the greater than the abyss or darkness in your life, from weakness comes strength.

Sophia
JUSTICE

Justice and injustice are thresholds for each other, and they are very relative. Let's divide it into two branches: that of the kingdom of God and that of the human kingdoms. Relates God, justice is closely linked to the sovereignty of Yahweh which is demonstrated through his commandments, a total of thirty according to my vision. It is a practical matter: Either you follow the norms of the kingdom of God or not and for those who refuse to see the greatness of these goals remains the lament of a soul having been lost. However, rebellious souls who manage to rise again at some point in life can firmly believe in the mercy of Yahweh, his holy father. God the father is a being of infinite assignments.

Human justice has its guidelines in every nation. Men over time strive to ensure peace and right on earth even though this does not always happen. This is due to outdated legislation, corruption, prejudice against minors and human failure itself. If you feel wronged as I have ever felt given your plea to God. He will understand the pain and ensure his victory at the right time.

Injustice in every respect is an evil of ancient and contemporary humanity. It has to be fought so that the righteous can have what is rightly yours. What can't happen is trying to do justice? Remember that it is not God to judge and condemn anyone.

"When I invoke you, answer me, God of my righteousness". (SM 4.2)

THE REFUGE AT THE RIGHT TIME

We are spiritual beings. At some point in our existence in heaven, we are chosen and incarnated in a human body at the moment of fertilization. The goal is to fulfill the mission by evolving with other human beings. Some with larger missions and others with smaller ones, but all with a function that the planet cannot give up.

Our first contact is within a family, and it is usually with these people that we live longer and throughout our lives. Even the children marrying the family bond are not extinguished.

With social contact, we have access to other different views of ours. That's exactly where the danger lies. Nowadays, we have a massive generation of young people seeking the evil side. They're teenagers and adults who don't respect their parents, worship the drug and to get it steal and even kill. Even so-called trusted people can hide a danger when they try to influence us to do evil. There's the other side too: Bombarded by falsehood, violence, bullying, prejudice, lying, disloyalty many disbelieve in humanity and close to new friendships. It's salutary to ponder that it's really hard to find reliable people, but if you're one of these lucky keep them on the right and left side of your chest for the rest of your life.

Exposed this, when you fall into some misfortune, turn to your true friends or close family and if you still do not find the support look for God *the refuge at the right time*. He's the only one who won't abandon him no longer as his situation is shaky. Give your pain and your faith on better days in the God of the impossible, and you will not repent.

"*In anguish you comforted me. Have mercy on me and listen to me* Prayer. (Psalm 4.2)

THE SEDUCTION OF THE WORLD VERSUS THE WAY OF GOD

The world is the great area where children of God and the devil work for their causes. As in any world lagging in terms of evolution, we live a bloody duality that people into groups that together form society.

Although we say that most people have good intentions, what you see is a virtualization of common sense. Most prefer the things of the world to the things of God. People crave power, money, compete for prestige, sink in unruly parties, practice exclusion and foment unruly, practice gossip and slander the other, prefer to climb the scale of hierarchy by defrauding, denouncing and passing over others. I, as Yahweh's representative, have no doubt that these people are not of God. They are daughters of the devil tares who will be burned mercilessly in the larvae of the abyss in the reckoning. It's no judgment, it's the reality in the plant-harvesting relationship.

If you have values and have faith in the forces of good, I invite you to be part of your father's kingdom. By renouncing the world, you will finally see the greatness and goodness of our God. A father who accepts you as you are and who loves you with love greater than your understanding reaches. Make your choice. Here everything is fleeting and beside us, you can experience what the word really means *"Full happiness."*

"O men, how long shall thou have his heart hardened, love vanity, and seek the lie? (Psalm 4:3).

GETTING TO KNOW YAHWEH

Yahweh is the most wonderful being there it. From my experience, I have known the face of this loving father who always wants our good. Then why not give him a chance? Give your crosses and hopes to him so that a strong hand can transform your life. I guarantee you won't be the same anymore. I sincerely hope that you will reflect these few words and make a definitive decision in your life. Furthermore, I'll be waiting for you. Good luck. I love you, brothers!

The righteous and the relationship with Yahweh
THE RELATIONSHIP WITH YAHWEH

Always thank your spiritual father for all the graces bestowed throughout his life. Feeling grateful and happy that Yahweh gave him life is an obligation. His name is holy and covered in glory in all parts of the world. In case of distress or need resort to it, and surely, it will open its ways showing a definitive solution to your problem.

Speaking of problems, many of them have as the cause the action of their enemies. Appeal with confidence to my father and anyone who wants evil will stumble. Know that God the father will always be by your side, just have more confidence in him. The righteous are always rested by the father. However, you must try an approach with your dislikes. Make your enemy a close and faithful friend or at least have a friendly relationship. An intrigue keeps the soul in darkness, away from divine action and no use complaining about the absence, you yourself have kept it away with your grudge and contempt towards others. Think about it.

Yes, God will love you and meet your expectations to the extent of the good you have done to others. Make sure that if you give it up completely, he will have his people battle for you in every internal and external war that occurs. He will be able to open the sea or destroy nations for his good because with faith you have turned to him.

He does so that he may sing his glory and in the dismay his soul join the chosen souls to rein with Jesus. The kingdom of God is being built little by little and most of its members are the poor and humble of heart. In this spiritual dimension there is only peace, happiness, faith, equality, cooperation, fraternity and love without limits among its members. Those who set out to follow the path of darkness, are now the lake of fire and brimstone, where they will be tormented day and night because of the severity of their sins.

This is called divine justice. Justice gives what everyone deserves by right and he does so in honor of the oppressed, the minorities, the suffering poor, all the little ones in the world who suffer subservient to the conservative elite. In addition to justice, divine mercy is found and impenetrable to any mind. That is why he is God, someone who will always be with open arms to receive his children.

WHAT YOU SHOULD DO

I met the divine father at the most difficult moment of my life, at an instant when I was dead and my hopes ran out. He taught me his values and rehabilitated me completely. He can do the same to you. All you have to do is accept the action of his glorious name in his life.

I follow some basic values: Love first, understanding, respect, equivalence, cooperation, tolerance, solidarity, humility, detachment, freedom and dedication to mission. Try to care for your life and do not slander the other because Yahweh judges' hearts. If someone hurts you, don't rethink, turn the other cheek and overcome your grudge. Everyone misses and deserves another chance.

Try to occupy your mind with work and leisure activities. Idleness is a dangerous enemy that can lead you to ultimate ruin. There's always something to do.

Also seek to strengthen your spiritual part, frequent your church frequently, and obtain counsel from your spiritual guide. It is always good to have a second opinion when we find ourselves in doubt about some decision to be made. Be prudent and learn from your mistakes and successes.

Above all, be yourself in all situations. No one cheats to God. Act in simplicity and always be faithful that God will entrust you even greater positions. Their greatness in heaven will be quantified in their servitude, the smallest of the earth will be graced with special places, close to the greater light.

I GIVE YOU ALL MY HOPE

Lord Yahweh, you who watch my efforts day and night, ask you for the guidance, protection, and courage to continue carrying my crosses. Bless my words and actions so that they are always good, beatified my body, my soul, and my mind. May my dreams come true no sea far as they may be. Do not allow me to turn to the right or to the left. When you die, give me the grace of living with the elect. Amen.

Friendship

True friend is the one who is with you in the bad times. He's the one who defends you with his soul and life. Don't be fooled. In times of bonanza, you will always be surrounded by people with the most varied interests. But in the dark times, only the true ones remain. Mostly your family. Those who imply so much and want their good are their true friends. Other people always get close because of advantages.

"You'll only eat honey bread with me if you eat grass with me." This true phrase sums up whom we should give true value to. The passing wealth attracts many interests and people transform. Know how to reflect on things. Who was with you impoverished? It's these people who really deserve your vote of confidence. Don't be fooled by the false passions that hurt. Analyze the situation. Would that someone have the same feeling for you if you were a poor beggar? Meditate on it, and you'll find your answer.

He who denies you in public is not worthy of his love. Anyone who is afraid of society is not prepared to be happy. Many people afraid of being rejected because of their sexual orientation reject their partners in public. This causes severe psychological disorders and persistent emotional pain. It's time to rethink your choices. Who really loves you? I'm certain this person who rejected you in public isn't among them. Take courage and change the trajectory of your life. Leave the past behind, make a good plan and move on. The moment you stop suffering for the other and take the reins of your life, your path will be lighter and easier. Don't be afraid and take a radical attitude. Only that can set you free.

Forgiveness

Forgiveness is extremely necessary to achieve peace of mind. But what does it mean to forgive? Forgiveness is not forgetting. To forgive is to end a situation that has brought you sadness. It's impossible to erase memories of what happened. This you will take with you for the rest of your life. But if you get stuck in the past, you'll never live in the present, and you won't be happy. Don't let the others take away your peace. Forgive me for moving forward and living new experiences. Forgiveness will finally set you free, and you will be ready to have a new vision of life. That man who made you suffer can't destroy your life. Think that there are other good men capable of providing you with good times. Have a positive attitude. Everything can get better when you believe it. Our positive vibrations affect our lives in such a way that we can triumph. Don't have negative or petty attitudes. This can lead to destructive results. Get rid of all evil that runs through your soul and filter only good. Just keep what adds good things to you. Believe me, your life will become better after this attitude.

Talk to your dislike frankly. Make your expectations clear. Explain that you've forgiven, but you won't give it a second chance. Reliving a loving past can be highly destructive for both. The best choice is to take a new direction and try to be happy. We all deserve happiness, but not everyone believes in it. Know how to wait for God's time. Be grateful for the good things you have. Keep searching for your dreams and your happiness. Everything happens at the right time. The creator's plans for us are perfect, and we don't even know how to understand. Give your life completely to God's designs and everything will work out. Embrace your mission with joy, and you will have pleasure in living. The feeling of forgiveness will transform your life in a way you never thought of and that bad event will only be an outdated obstacle. If you don't learn in love, you learn in pain. This is a saying applicable to that situation.

Finding your way

Each person has a particular and unique trajectory. There's no point in following any parameters. What is important is to research the possibilities. Having enough information is paramount to make a professional or loving decision. I believe that the financial factor should be considered, but it should not be essential in your decision. Often what makes us happy is not money. It is the situations and sensations of a certain area. Discover your gift, reflect on your future, and decide. Be happy with your choices. Many of them are definitive transforming our destiny. So, think well before the choices.

When we make the right choice, everything in our life flows perfectly. The right choices lead us to concrete and lasting results. But if you make a mistake in your decision, change your plans and try to get it right next time. You won't make up for lost time, but life has given you a new chance at success. We're entitled to every chance life gives us. We have the right to try as many times as we need. Who's never made a mistake in their lives? But always respect the feelings of others. Respect other people's decisions. Accept your failure. That's not going to diminish your capacity. Embrace your new start and don't sin again. Remember what Jesus said? We can even forgive, but you have to be ashamed and change your attitude. Only then will you be prepared to be happy again. Believe in your qualities. Have good ethical values and don't humiliate yourself to anyone. Make a new story.

How to live at work

Work is our second home, the extension of our happiness. It must be a place of harmony, friendship and complicity. However, this is not always possible. Why does this happen? Why am I not happy at work? Why am I persecuted? Why do I work so hard and I'm still poor? These and many other issues can be discussed here.

Work is not always harmonic because we live with different people. Each person is a world, has its problems, and it affects everyone around. That's where the fights and the disagreements happen. This causes pain, frustration and anger. You always dream of a perfect workplace, but when it comes to disappointment, it brings you discomfort. As a result, we were unhappy. Often, his work is his only financial support point. We have no option to resign even though we often want it. You cancel out and revolt. But he stays in the job out of necessity.

Why are we being chased by bosses and co-workers? There are many reasons: Envy, prejudice, authoritarianism, hopelessness. It marks us forever. This generates a feeling of inferiority and disillusionment. It's terrible to have to keep the peace when you want to scream to the world that's right. You do a perfect job, and you're not recognized. You don't get compliments, but your boss makes a point of criticizing you. Furthermore, you hit a thousand times, but if you make a mistake once you're called incompetent. Although I know that the problem is not in you, it generates consistent trauma sin your mind. You become a work object.

Why do I work so hard and I'm poor? That's got to be a reflection. We live in capitalism, a wild economic system in which the poor are exploited to generate wealth for the rich. This happens in all sectors of the economy. But being employed can be an option. We can undertake in almost all sectors with little money. We can create our business and be bosses of ourselves. This brings us incredible self-confidence. But nothing can be done without planning. We have to evaluate the positive and negative side so that we can decide which is the best way. We always need to have a background, but above all we need to be happy. Furthermore, we need to be proactive and become protagonists of our history. We need to find the "meeting point" of our needs. Remember that you are the only one who knows what is best for you.

Living with hard-tempered people at work

Often you find at work your worst enemy. That boring person who chases you and invents things to hurt you. Others don't like you for no apparent reason. This is so painful. Having to live with enemies is a terrible thing. It takes a lot of control and courage. We need to reinforce the psychological side to overcome all these obstacles. But there's also another option. You can switch jobs, request a transfer, or create your own business. Changing environments sometimes helps a lot the situation you're in.

How to deal with offenses? How to react in the face of verbal attacks? I don't think it's good to keep your mouth shut. That gives a false impression that you're a fool. React. Don't let anyone hurt you. You have to separate things. It's one thing for your boss to collect results from your work, and another thing quite different is to chase you. Don't let anyone choke your freedom. Be autonomous in your decisions.

Preparing to have an autonomous work income

To be able to leave work and be independent, we need to analyze the market. Invest your potential in what you like to do the most. It's great to work on what you like. You have to combine happiness with financial income. Work and make a good financial reserve. Then invest with planning. Calculate all your steps and steps. Research and consult experts. Be confident of what you want. With a way to go, everything will be easier for you.

If your first option doesn't work, reevaluate your path and persist in your goals. Believe in your potential and talent. Courage, determination, boldness, faith and persistence are the essential elements of success. Put God first and all other things will be added. Have faith in yourself and be happy.

Analyzing options of specialization in studies

Studying is essential for the labor market and for life in general. Knowledge aggregates and transforms us. Reading a book, taking a course, having a profession, and having a broad view of things helps us grow. Knowledge is our power against the attacks of ignorance. It takes us on a clearer and more precise path. Therefore, specialize in your profession and be a competent professional. Be original and create consumer trends. Free yourself from pessimism, take more risks and persist. Always believe in your dreams because they are your compass in the valley of darkness. We can do everything in him who strengthens us.

Research your area of expertise. Create learning mechanisms. Reinvent yourself. Becoming what you have always dreamed of may be possible. All it takes is one plan of action, planning and willpower. Create your success and you will be happy. Very successful for you.

How to live in the family
What is Family

Family is the people who live with you, whether they're related or not. It's the first family core you're a part of. Generally, this group is composed of father, mother and children.

Having a family is of fundamental importance for human development. We learn and teach in this little family nucleus. Family is our base. Without her, we're nothing. That's why this feeling of belonging to something fills the soul with the human being.

However, when we live with jealous or evil people, it can hinder our personal evolution? In this case, the following saying applies: "Better only than poorly accompanied". Man, also needs to grow, conquer his spaces and form his family. That's part of the natural law of life.

How to respect and be respected

The greatest rule of living in a family should be respect. Although they can live together, it does not entitle the other to meddle in their life. Reaffirm that position. Have your job, your room, your people things separately. Each family must have their personality, actions and desires respected.

Live together or leave home and have more privacy? Many young people ask themselves this question often. From my personal experience, it's only worth leaving the house if you have any support outside the home. Believe me, loneliness can be the worst of your enemies and mistreat you a lot.

I lived out for four months with the excuse that I'd be closer to work. But actually, I was trying to find love. I thought living in the big city would make it easier for me to search. But that's not what happened. People have become complicated in the modern world. Today, what prevails is materialism, selfishness and wickedness.

I used to live in an apartment. I had my privacy, but I felt totally unhappy. Furthermore, I've never been a young party, or drinking. Living alone doesn't appeal to me that much. In the end, I realized that my responsibilities had increased rather than diminished. So, I decided to go home. It wasn't an easy decision. I knew that they're ended my hopes of finding someone. I'm with the LGBT group. It's unthinkable that I get a boyfriend at home because my family is totally traditional. They'd never accept me for who I am.

I came home thinking about focusing on work. At the age of thirty-six, I'd never found a partner. He accumulated five hundred rejections and this increased every day. Then I asked myself: Why this need to find happiness in the other? Why can't I make my dreams come true on my own? All I had to do was have good financial support and I could enjoy life better. This thought of being happy next to someone is almost outdated these days. It rarely happens. So, I went on with my life with my projects. I'm a writer and a filmmaker.

Financial dependence

Knowing how to deal with the financial issue is paramount these days. Despite living as a family, everyone must have their livelihood. Many times, I had to help my family because I am the only one who has a steady job. But the situation got very difficult when they just waited for me. That's why I left the house, too. They had to wake up to reality. Helping is good when you have leftovers. But it's not fair that I'm working and other people enjoying my money more than I do myself.

This example shows how important awareness is. We have to separate things. Each one must seek to work. Everyone can survive. We need to be protagonists of our history and not depend on others. There are sick situations in today's world. That's not love. It's just financial interest. Being deceived with love will only bring suffering.

I understand that it is not easy to deal with some situations. But we must be rational. The son got married. Let him take over his life. Grandchildren to look after? Not at all. That's the parents' responsibility. You who are already in old age should enjoy life by traveling and doing pleasurable activities. You've fulfilled your role. Furthermore, you don't want to take care of other people's responsibility. This can be very damaging to you. Make an inner reflection and see what's best for you.

The importance of the example

When we talk about children, we talk about the future of the country. So, it's of the utmost importance that they have a good family base. Generally, they are the reflection of the environment in which they live. If we have a structured and happy family, the tendency is for young people to follow this example. That's why the saying is true: "He who is a good son is a good father." However, this is not a general rule.

We often have young rebels. Even though they have wonderful parents, they lean towards evil. In that case, don't feel guilty. You did your part. Every human being has his free will. If the child has chosen evil, it will bear the consequences. That's natural in a society. There is good and evil. This is a personal decision.

I chose good and today I am a pleased, honest and wholesome person. I am an example of persistence and hope towards my dreams. Furthermore, I believe in the values of honesty and work. Teach that to your children. Soothe good and reap the good. We are the fruit of our efforts, no more or less. Everyone has what they deserve.

End

www.ingramcontent.com/pod-product-compliance
Lightning Source LLC
LaVergne TN
LVHW020438080526
838202LV00055B/5248